George Washington

A Biography of an American President

Table of Contents

Introduction

Thank you for taking the time to read this book on George Washington!

This book covers the topic of George Washington, and will serve as a short biography of his incredible life and accomplishments. In the following chapters, you will discover how America's first President came to be, and just how much of an impact he had on the development of the United States.

You will learn about Washington's childhood, his time in the military, his politics, how he came to be the first President, what his personal life was like, and so much more!

As you'll soon find out, George Washington was a fascinating man whose impact is still felt today!

Once again, thanks for choosing this book, I hope you find it to be an enjoyable read!

Chapter 1: Who was George Washington?

One of the Founding Fathers of America, the highest ranking officer of the United States Army, the leader of the American Revolutionary War, the first President of the United States – one man was all of these. You will learn all about these remarkable achievements of George Washington, the Father of America, in this book.

Washington was an austere, stoic general who radiated immense power, pride, and gravitas. His presence inspired respect, admiration, and loyalty, but not warmth, friendship, and love. Washington appeared to his contemporaries as a reserved man.

He carefully curated this image, and he did this for many reasons. George Washington was a soldier, a politician, and an idealist. He understood that to serve his country, he had to be the unwavering man at the front lines. He understood that what the country needed wasn't another king, but a fearless leader. He understood that his actions would dictate the future of the country.

Accomplished men are often surrounded by myths and legends, and this was especially true for George Washington. He wanted to be a firm and steady hand guiding a newborn country. To do this, he believed that he must become a symbol. In the eyes of the public, George Washington was not a man, but a legend. He was the ideal for honesty, morality, and nationalism.

But because Washington was a legend, he was also unreachable and unknowable to many. As a result, many of his biographies have failed to capture his true essence. These biographies became a cold, factual, unfeeling dictation of names, dates, and places. But history is meant to be a teacher. To learn from George Washington, one must first know where he came from.

Chapter 2: The Washingtons

In the late seventeenth century, an Englishman settled in colonial Virginia. He was a successful man who played many roles throughout his life. He was a planter, trader, soldier, and politician. But history will remember him for his role in suppressing Native American uprisings. He met with five chiefs under the assumption of peace, and yet he killed them in cold blood. This earned him the title of *conotocarious*, or "town destroyer". This man was Lieutenant Colonel John Washington, George Washington's great-grandfather.

In 1658, John married a well-to-do woman named Anne Pope. Anne's father, Nathaniel Pope, was a wealthy and respectable colonel. Pope blessed the young couple with 700 acres of land, sparking John's interest in land-owning. By the end of his life, John owned almost 5,000 acres. He died in 1677 from typhoid fever, leaving behind three children: Lawrence, John II, and Ann.

As the eldest, Lawrence inherited most of his late father's sizable assets of land and slaves. But Lawrence wasn't particularly interested in plantation. Instead, he dedicated his life to the pursuit of power and influence. Lawrence became a law student, a soldier, and a captain. In 1685, he became a member of the House of Burgesses.

His ambition wasn't only confined to his professional life, but his personal life, too. He married Mildred Warner, who came from a respectable family. The Warners were members of the honorable *curia regis* or the king's council. This council served as the king's advisors on colonial matters.

Mildred bore him three children - John III, Augustine, and Mildred. When he died on February 1698, his estate was equally divided among his children. Augustine received a decent inheritance of a thousand acres of land and a few slaves. He took after his grandfather and became a planter and landowner.

Augustine married Jane Butler, with whom he had four children. Two of his children, Lawrence and Augustine, lived to adulthood. After his wife's death, he remarried a woman named Mary Ball. Mary bore him six children, four of which lived to adulthood. They were George, Betty, John Augustine, and Charles.

There are many commonalities among the Washington men in America. They were all driven, passionate, and ambitious men. All were prominent figures in their respective fields. The Washington men held positions of power. They were soldiers, sheriffs, burgesses, or justice of the peace. Through inheritance and marriage, the Washington family became wealthy and influential.

When George Washington was born, his family was part of America's middle class. His family wasn't lavish, but he was exposed to people whose families were. Still, he was a white, middle-class, land-owning man. He was born into privilege, blessed not only with means but with connections. These conditions shaped the kind of man that Washington became. It solidified his character, plagued his insecurities, and dictated his motivations.

Chapter 3: Birth and Early Life

George Washington was born to Augustine and Mary Ball Washington on February 22, 1732. He was from an affluent family, but he grew up in the provincial Westmoreland County in Virginia. His childhood was unlike that of the usual Virginian elite. Owing to his mother's influence, George was not spoiled. He had three younger siblings who he helped bring up. They also lived on a farm, which meant that he was also not a stranger to hard labor.

As a son

Mary Ball Washington was a strict, strong-willed, stubborn woman. She inherited the Ferry Farm from her husband upon his death. Owning and managing a farm was no easy task, especially without a husband. As a result, she relied on George for many tasks that were better-suited for adults.

Mary was a demanding disciplinarian who ruled with an iron fist. She required absolute obedience from her slaves and her children. As such, Mary and George had a complicated relationship, to say the least. When George was 11, his father died suddenly, and his upbringing was left to his mother.

At the time, his two older half-brothers, Lawrence and Augustine Jr., were in grammar school. George had expected to follow suit, but the family started having financial problems following the death of its patriarch. Unable to afford a formal education, George assumed the position as the man of the house.

As a child, George craved love, kindness, and attention. But this was impossible to receive from his hypercritical, self-centered mother. Even during his childhood, their interactions were frigid and formal. This was the most likely cause of George's reserved nature in his later life. George and Mary were very alike, yet very different. They were strong-willed, opinionated people. They prided themselves on their independence and work ethic. They even had the same talent for horseback riding.

But Mary was unconcerned with appearances, education, and social class. George was the exact opposite. He was meticulous about his personal style. He studied on his own and became a respected intellectual. He was an autodidact who studied math, land surveying, literature, philosophy, geography, and mapping. He enjoyed the life of privilege and status, and he conducted himself with grace and decorum.

The events of his childhood had a profound and damaging impact on George. He lacked formal education, and it caused him to feel insecure about his intellect for the rest of his life. In his later years, he would be presented with many responsibilities. He would humbly accept, but first he led with a disclaimer on his abilities. He was also raised by an overbearing mother, and it caused him to become an austere, reserved man. His upbringing made him hypercritical and unforgiving of his own mistakes. Lastly, he was from a middle-class family, but they often experienced financial instability. This caused him to feel self-conscious of his wealth, manners, graces, status, and social standing.

George found it particularly difficult to talk about his childhood and family life. Details about his early life were only recently discovered by historians. Through diligent research on his letters, correspondence, and accounts, they were able to paint a picture of his early life.

As a brother

George found solace in the company of his siblings. He was close to John Augustine, who he considered his constant boyhood companion. But it was his half-brother Lawrence who affected him the most. The young and impressionable George greatly admired Lawrence. He was a tall, handsome, and highly-educated man who exuded grace, class, and status. He served in the military as an adjutant in 1743 and in the House of

Burgesses as a burgess in 1744. He introduced young George to riches and ambition.

In 1743, Lawrence married a young woman named Anne Fairfax. She was the daughter of Colonel William Fairfax. The Washingtons belonged in the middle-class, but the Fairfaxes belonged to the elite. The colonel was a planter, a land agent, a commissioner, and a president of the governor's council. The marriage propelled Lawrence to the heights of the Virginian social class. By extension, George was also propelled to these new heights. In the company of Lawrence, he met patrons who saw his intellect as promising and took him under their care. One such patron was Colonel Fairfax himself.

As his own man

When George was 14, Lawrence and Colonel Fairfax agreed on a plan to free the boy from his mother. They wanted him to have a promising career in the Navy, and they got him a post as a midshipman. Mary considered seamen to be unruly, immoral savages, and so she forbade her son to go. This turned out to be a blessing in disguise, for George turned to real estate.

In his later years, he would say that his skill as a land surveyor was one of his most valuable assets. He excelled in surveying because of his many talents. He was skilled in numbers, he had a practical approach to problems, and he loved the outdoors. On top of his natural talent, he was also well-connected. The Fairfaxes' extensive network proved to be immensely helpful in furthering his career. By the time he was 17, he had received royal commissions and appointments. He had also started making serious money. He indulged in clothes, invested in land, and saved up for a plantation.

At a very young age, George was following the path of the Washington men. He was becoming wealthy, powerful, and successful. But with Washingtons, prosperity was diminished by frequent sickness and early death. His father, grandfather, and great-grandfather all died before they turned fifty. The same fate befell his beloved half-brother, Lawrence. Lawrence, then 34, had contracted tuberculosis. He died on July 26, 1752.

At this point, George had endured the deaths of his father, two brothers, and now, a half-brother. Given the nature of their relationship, it is fair to assume that George saw Lawrence as a father figure. He coped with his brother's death by living a life that he would have lived. And so, he abandoned his career as a land surveyor and he enlisted as a soldier.

Chapter 4: Virginia Militia

George Washington, if nothing else, was a man of determination. When he joined the militia, he relentlessly vied for his brother's post as adjutant. What he lacked in experience, he made up for in ambition and connection. At the tender age of 20, he was appointed as the adjutant of Northern Neck.

His six years of military service were in relation to the Ohio Company land conflict. This period was transformative to his military career, personal life, and nationalistic ideologies. His role in the Ohio Company land conflict prepared him for his role in the American Revolution.

In colonial America, private companies and individuals were awarded commissions for land speculation. They surveyed land and assessed its assets, features, and territory. After receiving approval from the parliament, they cut deals with the Native Americans. Once both parties agree on a price, the land was purchased, and then sold to settlers with a modest interest.

One such company was the Ohio Company of Virginia, founded by Lawrence and Augustine Washington. It was established with the intent of protecting the area against French expansion. The disputed territory was in the Forks of Ohio. The Forks are the convergence point of the rivers of Allegheny, Monongahela, and Ohio. Both Britain and France had staked their claim on the area, as it was a key location in the fur trade. If both empires planned to expand, they would first have to claim the Forks.

Envoy

Washington felt a sense of responsibility to his late brother's unfulfilled legacy. In October 1753, he was presented with the opportunity to honor his brother. He was appointed as an envoy by the Lieutenant Governor of Virginia, Robert Dinwiddie. At the time, Dinwiddie had just gone on the offense. He made a bold move by constructing British forts in the disputed territory. Washington's mission was two-fold. First, he needed to deliver a message to the French. The message was this: the British Empire claims this land, and they are willing to claim it by force. Second, he needed to earn the support of the Native American tribes.

This was a momentous opportunity for the young Washington. Very few colonial officers were entrusted with high-risk assignments, and certainly none as young as him. But he handled it like a leader. He braved the impossible storms and impassable lands. He diplomatically convinced the tribe leaders. He then delivered the message to the French commander, Captain Jacques Legardeur de St. Pierre. The captain then sent a message of his own. He made it clear that they were not threatened by the ultimatum, and that they would not vacate the area.

Washington delivered the captain's response to Dinwiddie in January 16, 1754. The general ordered him to submit a report of the mission. Not only did Washington write a detailed report of the events, he also described the French territory in great specificity. Because of his background as a surveyor, he was able to observe details that others would have missed.

In his report, he included information about the troops, weapons, defenses and fortifications. The intel he provided proved to be actionable, and it caused the French-Indian War. Despite his huge success, he was compensated with a measly fifty-pound reward.

Promotion

At the time, British officers believed that colonial officers were inferior. As a result, they were underpaid, overworked, and unrecognized. Washington was a proud man, and the insignificant reward injured his pride. He believed that he deserved more, and so he asked Dinwiddie for proper recognition. The lieutenant governor relented, and promoted him to lieutenant colonel.

For a brief, shining moment, Washington thought that the British finally had faith in him. Almost immediately, this was extinguished with the coming of Colonel Joshua Fry. Fry was leading an expedition, and he wanted Washington to be a part of his team. The young lieutenant felt insulted. His rank was higher than Fry's, but because he was British, he would have to submit to him. Reluctantly, Washington agreed.

Colonel Joshua Fry delegated 160 green troops to Washington. He instructed him to maintain a defensive position, unless the French fired first. Should this happen, he was explicitly ordered to retaliate and use deadly force. Meanwhile, the French had claimed the fort on the Forks of Ohio, renaming it Fort Duquesne.

While Washington had a mere 160 men, the French had a thousand. The latter had also replenished their supply of weapons and artilleries. Undeterred, the bold lieutenant requested assistance from nearby British territories. The colonies obliged, supplying him with hundreds of troops from Maryland and Pennsylvania.

Great Meadows

By early May, the tension was rising. Neither party had yet acted aggressively, but both parties anticipated it. There was a hint of fear and paranoia in the air, aggravated by a message that Washington received. According to report, a small group of French troops had advanced on their territory.

The young lieutenant acted as he was ordered, and maintained a line of defense at the Great Meadows. However, he had received further news about the French group. Apparently, they were skulking about and ready to strike. Another report warned of an impending French attack. In Washington's point of view, this supported the former intel, and he decided to go on the offense.

Washington tracked down the group to a secluded camp and encircled the area. There is some dispute as to what happened next, and no one is certain who fired the first shot. What is certain are the numbers: ten dead Frenchmen, twenty one captured, all under fifteen minutes. This was, however, far from a victory; one of the dead men turned out to be a peace envoy.

Ensign Joseph Coulon de Villiers, Sieur de Jumonville, was carrying a diplomatic letter.

There was no question that the French would retaliate, and that lives would be lost. Washington, however, stood his ground. According to him, if the group had purely diplomatic intentions, they would not have acted in a cloak-and-dagger manner. Another complication was the death of his superior, Colonel Fry. Suddenly, Washington became the highest-ranking officer. He held the fate of the entire Virginian regiment in his hands.

Fort Necessity

Washington was a 22-year-old lieutenant colonel with only two years of military experience. He didn't yet look like the respected general that most people recognize. He stood tall at six foot two inches, had a red head of hair, and the build of a strong equestrian. He was well-known for his seriousness and stoic temperament, but what he hid was his stubbornness. Faced with impossible odds, he stood his ground. He quickly constructed a defensive fort from what little materials they had. It was ironically named Fort Necessity.

Fort Necessity turned out to be one of Washington's most monumental failures. A large group of French soldiers led by the dead envoy's brother descended on the fort with a hail of bullets. The attack wiped out one-third of his men, and Washington surrendered. The scandal stoked the already heated threat of war.

His reputation took a hit when French newspapers painted him as a juvenile leader. Fortunately, American newspapers published his version of accounts. His stellar record remained untarnished, and his bravery and conduct were revered by the press. He was also publicly lauded by members of the House of Burgesses.

Washington prided himself on being a circumspect man. He always tried to look at situations logically and strategically. At the Great Meadows and Fort Necessity, he acted recklessly, and he knew it. The Virginia Regiment was dissolved, and he resigned in 1754.

Return

Throughout his illustrious, eventful life, Washington has lived in many places. Yet there is but one place that he truly called his home. After his resignation, he went back to Mount Vernon. He began renovations to make the house more presentable and the land more profitable. He designed the building himself, following trends from European architecture. After serving many years in the militia, Washington enjoyed this peaceful life. However, his hiatus was cut short with the arrival of Major General Edward Braddock.

Braddock was sent to America with the sole purpose of reclaiming Fort Duquesne. Despite the fiasco of Fort Necessity, Braddock recognized Washington's expertise, and so he appointed him as his aide. Braddock was a brash, prideful, and stubborn man. He believed that English officers were superior, and colonial officers were adequate at best.

Washington would offer his advice, as was his professional duty, but his words fell on deaf ears. One such advice was to divide the platoon into two. The first would march ahead and the second would carry the bulk of supplies, following at a later time. Braddock ignored his counsel; as a result, the men moved at a sluggish pace of two miles a day.

Eventually, Braddock listened. But en route to Fort Cumberland, Washington fell ill with dysentery. He was plagued with a severe headache, high fever, and violent diarrhea. The major general ordered him to stay with the slower group, as he was too weak to ride on horseback. He reluctantly complied.

Braddock's fault was in never questioning his perceived superiority of the British ways. He was accustomed to their weapons, their terrains, and their tactics. But he failed to take into account that he was up against something different. This oversight allowed him to be blindsided, and he led his army straight into an ambush.

The French had struck an alliance with the Indians, and they engaged in a clandestine attack. Upon reaching the fort, the French and Indians opened fire on the British. The British troops attempted to retaliate, but the enemy had already disappeared. What was especially disorienting was the enemy's terrifying war cries. In all the chaos and confusion, the British did not realize that they had already been surrounded. When they did, it was too late.

The second group, including Braddock and Washington, had walked into a war zone. Of the two thousand troops, five hundred men had been killed, and another five hundred were injured. In desperation, Braddock ordered Washington to retrieve two cannons. To do so, Washington would have to cross the entire battlefield and ride uphill with no cover and no backup. Given the cannon's location and Washington's condition, this was a near impossible task.

But, in an extraordinary feat of willpower, he followed his orders. He incurred no damage but four bullet holes in his shirt and two in his hat. When his horse was shot out from under him, he simply dismounted and rode another one. Braddock was not as fortunate; during the battle, he was shot in the shoulder, and the bullet was lodged in his lung. Washington took Braddock to safety, but he eventually succumbed to his injuries, dying four days later.

The expedition was a humiliating defeat, more so for Washington than anyone else. Unlike Braddock, he was familiar with the French and Indians. He had expected their moves at every turn, and he forewarned Braddock. Washington resented the late general's ignorance and stubbornness. By the end of the battle, he was already disillusioned with the supposed superiority of the British.

Commander-in-chief

But the failed expedition and Braddock's death only elevated Washington's reputation. When word spread of his conduct under fire, he was instantly sensationalized. The stories inspired a powerful mental image. Imagine a young George Washington riding straight into the battlefield, narrowly avoiding the bullets intended for him. This earned him not only love and respect from the American public. It also earned him a promotion to the position of commander-in-chief of Virginia.

His conduct as a commander precluded his later conduct as a general and a president. He was a strict disciplinarian who enforced strict rules. He forbade gambling, drinking, and even swearing. He frequently doled out punishment against deserters. Nevertheless, he had earned the respect and admiration of his officers and subordinates.

Washington was given many responsibilities as the supreme commander of all Virginian forces. He was tasked with protecting the frontier and the training of the Virginian army. Washington also fiercely advocated the reclamation of Fort Duquesne. At the time, his interests and ambitions extended beyond his current post in the military.

For the past year, he had been vying for a royal commission. A royal commission would make him eligible for land grants and military privileges. Given his many accomplishments and sacrifices, he felt entitled to it; yet, his requests were repeatedly rejected. And so, he turned his sights to the House of Burgesses.

He ran twice - first in December 1756, and again in 1758. His first campaign was a disaster. Washington took great care to appear humble, so he joined the race at the last minute. This tactic did not work; he only received 9 votes. Always a self-improving man, he learned from his mistakes and ran again two years later. He enlisted the help of his friends to campaign for him, as he was too busy at the frontier. His recent actions in Braddock's expedition also helped with the publicity. By a landslide, Washington won in absentia.

His last memorable act in the military was in November 1758. Finally, he was presented with the opportunity to capture the elusive Fort Duquesne. Washington received intel that the fort was suffering from a shortage of men, food, and supplies. With 2,500 men, Washington marched on Fort Duquesne, only to be welcomed by the sight of it up in flames. As it turns out, the alliance of the French and Native Americans had been dissolved. With depleted resources, it would be impossible to defend the fort. Rather than surrender it to the British, they burned it instead. This defeat finally convinced Washington to resign. In December 1758, Washington stepped down from his post as commander-in-chief. This concluded his service for the Virginian militia.

Chapter 5: Personal Life

Washington's contemporaries viewed him as a man of quiet dignity. He kept his private affairs away from the public eye and rarely, if at all, talked about his personal life. When he did, he talked about it in broad terms. He designed and constricted himself to be viewed only as a leader, and not a man. Despite his secretive exterior, Washington was passionate, affectionate, and loving. He valued his relationships, his marriage, and his family.

Romances

Washington's first true romance was Sally Fairfax, the wife of George William Fairfax. George William was the son of his patron, Colonel Fairfax, and he was his oldest friend. Yet, Washington and Sally had always felt a strong connection. This was due in large part to their common interests. For a man who thirsted for knowledge, Sally was an oasis.

She introduced him to a wealth of knowledge that his mother deprived him of. She taught him philosophy, history, literature, and French. As she was a well-to-do woman, she was immersed in the world of the Virginian elite. And so, she also taught him social graces, manners, conversation, and even dancing. She was, in his eyes, the ideal woman, and despite, or perhaps because of the fact that she was married, he fell in love with her.

In their early years, they enjoyed a clandestine flirtatious relationship. Their letters would test the line between proper and improper. Even when Washington was in Ohio, he would write her intimate letters. Sometimes he was so bold that he even deigned to omit her husband. But whenever Washington acted too explicit and forward, Sally would become cold. This suggests that Sally merely enjoyed his intimate attention and faraway affection.

When Washington returned to Mount Vernon in 1758, he began to work on the house and the estate. He thought about his future and considered starting a family. In early March, he met a wealthy widow by the name of Martha Dandridge Custis. Martha was married to a rich planter, Daniel Parke Custis. She bore him two children, John "Jacky" and Martha "Patsy".

When she was widowed at the age of 25, Martha inherited her late husband's considerable estate. It consisted of 17,500 acres, 300 slaves, and 5 plantations. Their courtship was rapid, characteristic of a widow and a military man on leave. Within a few weeks after their meeting, the young couple got engaged.

At the time of their engagement, Washington still harbored feelings for Sally. Not wanting to have regrets, he sent her a letter confessing his love. It should be noted that the letter was dated on the eve of his attack on Fort Duquesne. The timing suggests that his mindset was that of a man contemplating his mortality. It was also his intent, should he make it out of Fort Duquesne alive, to wed Martha. Despite being a profession of love, the letter marked the end of their romantic relationship. Their friendship, however, stood the test of time.

Marriage

Washington did make it out of Fort Duquesne, and on January 6, 1759, he married Martha Dandridge Custis. She took his last name and was theretofore known as Martha Washington. His marriage to Martha elevated not only his wealth, but social standing. From the eyes of a distant observer, the pairing could seem purely practical.

However, it was obvious to anyone who saw them that the couple was perfectly suited for each other. They greatly enjoyed subtle elegance, but steered away from vulgarity. Both genuinely derived pleasure and felicity from each other's presence. For him, Martha served as his home, the strong foundation in his ever tumultuous life.

As previously mentioned, Washington often spoke of love and marriage in broad terms. While he didn't reveal anything specific, his enthusiasm about the subject speaks volumes. He wrote to younger relatives, freely giving advice on matters of love and women. In one such letter, he wrote that one must choose a strong companion over a passionate fling.

This was an obvious allusion to the choice he made with Martha and Sally. He also valued the institution of marriage, and theirs was a particularly strong one. Long after the passion had gone, the warmth, trust, friendship, tenderness, and love remained.

Martha also set the precedence for the responsibilities of a first lady. At the time, the post wasn't official; the term wasn't even coined until after her husband's presidency. Still, she gracefully played the role. She often engaged in philanthropic acts and visited encampments during the revolution. During her husband's campaign, Martha also played the sociable hostess and the dutiful wife.

Family

Washington never fathered a child himself, but the Mount Vernon house was never lacking in children. He was a loving father to his stepchildren, Jacky and Patsy. Although he loved Jacky like a son, their relationship was strained.

Washington often said that he knew how to train men but not how to raise boys. Because Jacky was a particularly unruly boy, one might think that Washington would assume the role of a disciplinarian. However, Martha had already lost two children and was protective of Jacky and Patsy. Washington kept his distance from the delicate issue of his upbringing. But he greatly contributed to his education and enrolled him in King's College.

Patsy, on the other hand, was especially dear to him; even as he considered himself a disciplinarian, he always maintained a soft spot for the girl. He often doted on her, spoiling her with clothes, jewelry, and musical instruments. He also ensured that she had a well-rounded education. Unfortunately, when she turned twelve, she developed a seizure disorder.

The wealthy family tried all kinds of treatment to no avail. Five years later, after dinner, Patsy went up to her room, and had a particularly violent episode. Washington rushed to her room and held her, until two minutes later, she passed away.

Upon his sister's death, Jacky became disinterested in his studies and he left university. In the spring of 1773, he got engaged to Eleanor Calvert of the wealthy Calvert family of Maryland. As Washington did not have the chance to go to college, Jacky's decision disappointed him.

While he did not expressly forbid the marriage, neither did he strongly approve of it. It took him some time, but he came around and took the couple in his own house. They would later have four grandchildren. Despite their problems and differences, Washington's love and fondness for Jacky never diminished.

Chapter 6: After the Militia

After his military service, Washington's life was of domestic bliss and entrepreneurial undertakings. The next years of his life inspired a brief moment of peace and happiness. For the time being, he enjoyed life as a civilian, a stepfather, a planter, a host, and a businessman.

Properties

When he left for Braddock's exhibition, he was in the middle of rehabilitating his estate. In his absence, he asked his brother, John, to manage Mount Vernon. However, he arrived to see his home in a state of neglect, and so he revived the renovation. Washington personally supervised the repairs to his estate.

He also sought to improve the tobacco plantation. He tried experimenting with different techniques, but growing tobacco proved to be difficult. For the first six years, there were little to no yields. Those that were harvested were of low quality, thus fetching low prices. Despite the fact that the crop was hemorrhaging money, he continued to plant it. This was in part due to his agreement with a British creditor by the name of Robert Cary.

Cary managed his export of tobacco and import of goods from London. At the time, it was common for Virginian landowners to be wealthy in properties, real estate, and investments, but poor in cash. This was also the case with Washington. He found Cary's services unreliable, yet he continued to do business with him. This was because of Cary's generous line of credit.

Although he considered himself a practical man, Washington had dangerous spending habits. He spent a fortune importing clothes, furniture, books, and even a carriage at one point. Soon, he began to incur debt; by the 1760's, he owed Cary two thousand pounds. Washington was an extremely proud man. It could not have been easy for him to be so deeply indebted to someone, and to a British man no less.

There was a morbid pattern in Washington's life. The deaths of those closest to him ended up benefitting him in one way or another. Lawrence's death started his military career, making him eligible for land grants. Anne's death left him Mount Vernon. Braddock's death earned him a promotion to commander-in-chief. It even propelled him to great fame. This pattern continued with his beloved stepdaughter's death.

Martha's first husband, Daniel Parke Custis, was an extremely wealthy man. He bequeathed one-third of his assets to his widow, and one-third to each of his children. When Washington married Martha, he assumed responsibility of the Custis estate. After Patsy died, her assets reverted to Washington; with this cash influx, he was able to pay off his debt.

Civilian Life

Despite his finances, Washington still relished in the privileges of his status. He spent his brief civilian life pursuing other interests and recreational activities. He was a strong, active man, and he enjoyed horse-riding, fishing, and hunting. Washington also appreciated the finer things in life. He loved dancing and going to the theatre. He was also fond of hosting and entertaining people in his home in Mount Vernon.

In this period of his life, he felt at home in his role as a husband, a step-father, and a planter. But, he was a civic-minded man who still felt a deep need to help his community; and he did this in every way he could. On a small scale, he was generous to his friends, relatives, and anyone who showed up at his doorstep. On a larger scale, he helped people through his position at the House of Burgesses. He contributed his military expertise to settle matters related to soldiers, veterans, and land grants.

It was clear that as best he could, Washington tried to live a moral life. Interestingly, he lived during a time when morality was linked to religious beliefs. And yet, he never explicitly confirmed his religion. In 1762, he was a vestryman and a churchwarden to an Anglican church. He performed his duties, attended mass, and went above and beyond to help the less fortunate. Still, his religious belief was a frequent subject of debate, and for valid reasons.

First, he always spoke of god and religion vaguely. He skillfully avoided specifying anything beyond "author of our being". Second, he belonged to multiple congregations. He was often seen attending mass in other denominations. Third, he detested anything that could be interpreted as zealous and reverent behavior - even if it was for god.

There are many possible explanations for this ambiguity - the most convincing of which is his privacy. Given what is known about the man, if he truly believed in god, this belief would be private. He would not use his faith to boast of his religiosity, much less use it to leverage for political support. This theory is bolstered by the fact that many of his good deeds were done anonymously.

Washington believed that a truly generous act need not be heralded nor repaid. Whatever his religion was, it is indisputable that Washington had an internal moral compass. To the best of his ability, he tried to live in accordance with what he believed was moral, ethical, and just.

Rebellion

On February 10, 1763, Britain and France signed the Treaty of Paris. The treaty marked the end of the French-Indian War, with Great Britain as the victor. Per the treaty, all French territories in North America were awarded to Great Britain. This resulted in freedom and safety for the Americans, and opportunity of expansion for the British. However, this victory came at a great financial cost. The military expenses from the war amounted to almost £210 million, or £40 billion today.

The mother country believed that since America shared the spoils of the war, it should also share the expenses. To solve the financial crisis, the British implemented drastic measures. These measures included the removal of defensive troops and the implementation of taxes. In 1765, the Stamp Law was passed.

Under this law, all printed paper products were taxed. This included books, newspapers, magazines, folios, textbooks, and legal documents.

Ranging from one penny to ten pounds, the tax was relatively small. The repercussions, however, were not. The fine print of the law sent a message: the taxation of paper was the taxation of information. The message was supported by the fact that the tax primarily affected college textbooks and legal documents. This suggests that Britain intended to limit the number of American professionals. After all, America was still a colony, and colonies are subject to revolt. It was in Britain's best interest to keep Americans uninformed and uneducated.

At first, Americans reacted to the Stamp Act with pleas, appeals, and protests. They expressed their discontent to colonial courts and congresses. But the British parliament responded by dissolving these courts. For the Americans, the crime was clear: taxation without representation. This revolutionary slogan meant that colonists were being taxed as much as regular subjects. However, they did not partake in the benefits, nor did they have a voice in the Parliament. Soon, the tension was palpable, and the threat of rebellion became imminent. The Stamp Act was repealed in 1766.

The relief, however, was short-lived. In the following year, the Townshend acts were enacted. Instead of paper, items like paint, glass, lead, and tea were taxed. Again, these unreasonable laws were met with anger, dissent, and threats of boycott. The Townshend duties eventually led to the Boston Massacre of 1770, and the Boston Tea Party of 1773.

At the time, the duality of opinions among colonists was a common phenomenon. It was the stringent effect of colonization. Colonists opposed the Parliament and its laws, but they worshipped the king. As a colonial officer, Washington had experienced this firsthand. He experienced the duality, colonial mentality, and the gradual disillusionment towards Britain. He risked his life many times to defend Britain and its territory. Yet all he got in return were ill treatment, little reward, and no acknowledgement. This resulted in George Washington becoming one of the first radical separatists.

Chapter 7: Commander of the Revolution

Eve of War

Even with widespread discontent, a revolution cannot happen overnight. The twelve-year gap between the Stamp Act and the American Revolution indicated two things. First, it showed the hesitation of Americans towards complete separation. Second, it showed the disunity of the colonies. The latter is interesting as it was orchestrated by the British.

They believed that in the event of a rebellion, it would be easier to defeat them if they were disassociated. This tactic proved effective. There have been very few reasons for the colonies to interact, much less act towards a common goal.

This started to change when the First Continental Congress convened in September 4, 1774. It should be noted that this act of defiance, even a nonviolent one, was the result of a long, arduous process. At least for a high-ranking colonial officer that had served the British agenda, it was the result of a series of small revolutions.

The twelve-year gap was eventful for Washington, to say the least. He had become a strong opponent of the British rule. He advocated for the boycott of British goods and called for direct action. He had begun to fight not only against taxation, but also for America's abstract right of freedom.

Eager to do more, he went to the House of Burgesses. He appealed for the right to protest and for leniency towards offenders. The following day, the governor abruptly stopped the assembly, then demanded the immediate dissolution of the burgesses.

Washington was fuming, but instead of acting rashly, he opted for diplomacy. On July 17, he drafted the Fairfax Resolves. Under the Fairfax resolves, he stated that Virginians will only be taxed by Virginians. They will only follow laws that are approved by people that they approved. The resolves also drew attention to two things. First, it called to put an end to the importation of slaves. Second, it emphasized the need for provincial defense.

The former was one of his earliest public anti-slavery notions. This was one of the earliest signs that he found slavery incompatible with their fight for freedom. The latter resulted to the formation of Virginia's independent militia. It comprised of volunteers led by Washington himself.

Instead of pacifying the troubled colonies, the British only doubled down. As a response to the Boston Tea Party, they passed what would later be called the Intolerable Acts. These acts demanded for the full repayment of the destroyed merchandise. The disbanded burgesses came together and formed the Virginian Convention. This was the last step before the First Continental Congress. The congress was of utmost importance. It is first time that twelve of thirteen colonies met to discuss appropriate action. The delegates included prolific activists, lawyers, statesmen, and politicians - John and Samuel Adams, Patrick Henry, Samuel Chase, and John Jay. The goal of the congress was threefold:

1. To present a united front by collectively boycotting British goods.

2. To demand the repealing of the Intolerable Acts.

3. To amplify the call for action to form voluntary militias.

The First Continental Congress was an unmitigated success. It concluded with a call for a second assembly, which was to be held in May 10, 1775, in Philadelphia, Pennsylvania.

Before the second congress, British General Gage had planned to arrest Samuel Adams and John Hancock. They were to be tried for treason and conspiracy. Gage tracked them to a safe house in Lexington, Massachusetts. He had also uncovered the location of weapons and artillery a few miles away in Concord.

Unbeknownst to the general, Adams and Hancock were tipped off and they fled to safety. What was supposed to be an arrest and seizure turned into the battle of Lexington and Concord. It was the first bloodshed of the American Revolutionary War.

It was a bloody battle between redcoats and a militia group called the Minute Men. It was a decisive victory for the latter. This incident marked the revolution's transition from ink to blood. When the first shot was fired on April 19, Washington knew that it was time to prepare for war.

The General

Following the battle of Lexington and Concord, the Second Continental Congress reconvened. This time, it was to officially declare America's independence on July 4, 1776. The congress also thought it was time to discuss matters of war. Naturally, the delegates turned to Washington.

He was largely instrumental in matters of recruitment, defense, weaponry, and strategies. Washington was not well-versed in the art of public speaking. But when he spoke, people listened. And even in his calm, collected exterior, there was a palpable rage against the British.

By June 14, Massachusetts, Rhode Island, Connecticut, Pennsylvania, Maryland, Virginia, and New Hampshire had raised ten companies. Washington was unanimously elected as the commander-in-chief of the Continental Army. At that point, he had had sixteen years of experience as a politician, and he had extensive knowledge of what it meant to be a public figure. Through small actions, he became a symbol. He did not actively lobby for the position, nor did he allow congress to pay him for his services. It sent the message that his motive wasn't power or money; his motive was freedom for all.

In June, he left Philadelphia and journeyed north to Boston. En route, he received a message that General William Howe had captured Breed's Hill. Washington headed to Massachusetts to assume control of the Continental Army. He led by convincing his troops to set aside their differences and come together.

He believed that the war could only be won by uniting all colonies into one national identity. He inspired the loyalty of his soldiers by sending a message that he was one of them, and that he would fight with them. He fulfilled this promise during the first six years of his post. He directed the Siege of Boston, New York, New Jersey, Trenton, Princeton, and Philadelphia.

The Americans were up against the greatest, most powerful empire in the world. They struggled with lack of men, food, supplies, and ammunition. The state of their resources put them in a position of extreme disadvantage. Because of this, Washington and his army lost more battles than they won. Nevertheless, he never lost sight of the agenda. After all, he was both a politician and a general, and he understood both sides of the war.

What he lacked in resources, he made up for in strategy; this was the case in the Siege of Yorktown on October 9, 1781. Washington was up against General Cornwallis, who was based in Yorktown. It was a strategic, defensive position; Yorktown was protected against land forces, but not against naval forces. Unbeknownst to the British, the Americans had struck an alliance with the French. The French contributed manpower, food, supplies, and ships. The Americas now had ample resources to overpower the defenses of Yorktown. With a series of maneuvers, Washington blocked Cornwallis' reinforcements. He feigned an attack in New York, causing the latter to dispatch soldiers en masse. Yorktown became undermanned and undefended. Before he knew it, Yorktown was captured, and Cornwallis surrendered.

On the other side of the Atlantic, Benjamin Franklin was in Paris, serving as a peace envoy. Upon receiving word of the Yorktown victory, he knew that the war was won. He strong-armed the British into signing a peace treaty. With one fell swoop, the American Revolutionary War was over, and America was free.

After the American Revolutionary War, Washington disbanded his army and resigned as commander-in-chief. He returned to his private life in Mount Vernon, firm in his belief that winning the war was his last act of service for his country.

Chapter 8: Politics

If this were a story, winning the American Revolutionary War was as happy as endings go. The humble hero returned to his life in the province, and it was the ever after that he dreamed of. However, it turns out that building a new nation was much more complicated than fighting for it.

Constitutional Convention

Following the war, the colonies reverted back to its disunited state. It was ruled over by a congress that had no actual power to implement laws. Washington, believing his part was over, had taken a step back. But his respite from the public life was not totally politically idle. To his friends, he confided what he envisioned for the future of America. Washington believed that the country should have a central federal government under which all the colonies should unite. Currently, America was a house of cards. It was struggling under the weight of its debts and lawlessness. It wasn't a country; it was an estranged group of individualistic states who felt like they didn't owe anything to each other.

Washington had his reasons for not getting involved. His health was worsening, his estate was struggling, and he wanted to spend time with his family. However, he knew something had to be done. His conscience, and perhaps his pride, did not allow him to ignore the state of his country. Washington was elected as a delegate, later president, of the 1787 Philadelphia convention. The convention met to amend the Articles of Confederation. Washington was well-suited for the leadership role. He was experienced in matters of politics and war. He was an impartial, fair-minded, and attentive listener. He inspired unity and harmony amongst the delegates.

The convention did not start smoothly. There were many points of debate and contention. The main problems were the division of power and proportionality of representation for each state.

The delegates all agreed that the new nation should not be like the monarchial, tyrannical British. However, due to their differences, it still became a lengthy process. Finally, the convention came to a compromise and a final draft. In the Senate, there would be one representative per state. In the House of Representatives, there would be an amount of representatives proportional to the population of each state. They also decided that the government should be divided into three separate branches - executive, legislative, and judicial. This system removes power from any one man, and it holds him accountable to other branches. The amended constitution was approved and signed by 39 of the 42 delegates, and thus, a republic was born.

With the adoption of the new constitution, the country needed a president. Washington was the obvious choice because of his military achievements, political skills, and contributions to the founding of the country. He was respected by his contemporaries and revered by the public. Washington, however, was unconvinced that his skills were adequate to run a country. At his age, he had become jaded by power. He contemplated the presidency with reluctance and wariness. But, as always, when necessary, he heeded the call of his country. The Electoral College held an election on February 4, 1789, and with 69 votes, he won unanimously. George Washington, the first president of the United States, was inaugurated on April 30, 1789.

First Term

History views Washington as one of the greatest presidents of America. At the time, however, every aspect of his presidency was met with controversy. Americans were worried that the new republic would eventually descend to anarchical autocracy. Washington's humility and reluctance served as a cold comfort to some; still, his actions were watched closely.

The presidency proved to be a massive undertaking, one that he could not tackle alone. His first task as president was to establish departments in the executive branch. In an advising capacity, he enlisted the help of Tobias Lear, David Humphreys, and William Jackson. Washington also appointed members of his cabinet: Thomas Jefferson as secretary of state, Alexander Hamilton as secretary of treasury, Henry Knox as secretary of war, and Edmund Randolph as the attorney general. This action was complemented by the Judiciary Act of 1789, which established positions, districts, and departments in the judiciary branch. The appointment of Supreme Court judges fell to Washington, and he nominated John Jay as chief of justice.

Although he strongly opposed it, the constitution was amended under the Washington administration. The amendment of 1789 had included the Bill of Rights. Washington thought that the rights of Americans did not have to be explicitly written in the constitution. Under pressure from critics, he eventually relented. The inclusion of the Bill of Rights convinced the last colonies, North Carolina and Rhode Island, to officially be a part of the United States.

His next task was to create a federal revenue stream. One of the challenges of the new republic was its crippling debt. Washington believed that by clearing America's debts, its foreign relations will be more robust. Hamilton, the secretary of treasury, shared this belief. In January of 1790, he published The Report of Public Credit. According to his paper, the country owed an alarming total of $69 million to states and other nations. Fortunately, he also came up with a solution to remedy this – taxes, tariffs, and customs. He also proposed the federal government to assume state debts, to create the official American currency, and to establish the first central bank in America. Hamilton's actions, under Washington's guidance, set the precedence for America's economic and foreign policy.

Hamilton's taxation plan had a provision of excise tax for whiskey. This felt all too familiar for the recently emancipated Americans. The plan was strongly opposed by the public; nevertheless, the whiskey tax was passed. The opposition quickly turned violent, leading to the Whiskey Rebellion of 1791. It was the first uprising of the Washington administration, and the president intended to solve it peacefully. However, after many warnings and negotiations, it became clear that the situation could only be resolved by a show of force. Washington personally assumed command of a small army 13,000 strong, and marched to the militia's encampment at Carlisle.

This was a bluff on his part, as he still believed that bloodshed of other Americans was unnecessary. It worked; almost instantly, the opposition was intimidated into disbanding. Washington exercised leniency for the prisoners, but executed two rebel leaders. Although the Whiskey Rebellion was prevented, it ultimately led to Hamilton quitting his post.

Washington's first term was an unmitigated success. He enjoyed popularity amongst his constituents and loyalty amongst his cabinet. However, the presidency was no easy job, and the stress took its toll on his health. He began experiencing blinding headaches and intense rheumatoid arthritis. At one point, he developed a growth in his thigh. It was unconfirmed whether the growth was cancer or an abscess formed by infection. Soon, the pain grew unbearable, and it needed to be surgically removed. Surgery then was not yet as refined as it is now. It was an extremely painful procedure that left him bedridden for weeks. This incident also coincided with her mother's rapidly declining health. Mary Ball Washington died from breast cancer on August 25, 1789.

Second Term

Because of overwhelming stress and medical issues, Washington wanted to retire after his first term. However, Adams and Jefferson, worried about the country's delicate state, begged him to stay. Washington agreed on the condition that if elected, it would be his last term. Come the Election of 1793, he was unanimously re-elected as president.

If possible, his second term was more tumultuous than the first. At this point, it had become indefensibly inconsistent that a free nation makes its wealth on the backs of slaves. During this term, there were two laws passed regarding slavery – the Fugitive

Slave Act of 1793 and the Slave Trade Act of 1794. The former allowed for the recapturing of escaped slaves by any means necessary, while the latter put an immediate stop to the importation of new slaves. The majority of the men in the Congress, the Senate, and even the president himself, were slave-owners. As such, these two laws were hypocritical, contradictory half-measures. They tainted the American ideology of liberty, equality, and fraternity.

While his first term was focused on laying the groundwork of a new republic, his second term was focused on protecting it. One of the growing threats to the country was the rift between Hamilton and Jefferson. At first, the two had a respectful, cordial relationship, but they grew apart because of Hamilton's economic system in 1791. They began to form two different ideologies, Jefferson's Democratic-Republican Party and Hamilton's Federalist Party.

Hamilton's party was the first American political party. It reflected its founder's vision for America. Hamilton strived to make the country a military and economic superpower, but this comes with a great cost. In his idea of a centralized government, the citizens lose representation. It teetered on the brink of being a monarchy.

Jefferson's party, on the other hand, was founded on republicanism. It was an ideology that believed that the power should belong to the people. Republicanism was established as a response to Hamilton's federalism. He viewed it as a threat to democracy and the very heart of the country.

Washington tried to reconcile the two men, but the movement had already gained traction. As an advocate for unity, the fact that the irreparable division of America happened on his watch was something that Washington would regret for his remaining years.

Another challenge to the administration was the growing tension in America's national and foreign relations. That was the time when the Northwest Indian War and the French Revolutionary Wars happened.

The former had already been happening long before Washington's presidency. Under the Treaty of Paris, the British were ordered to vacate all North American territories. They conceded most forts, but they remained in the Northwest Territory.

Washington wanted to resolve the dispute with ceasefires and treaties. He sent a thousand men as a show of force, but they were greatly outnumbered. As it turns out, the British struck an alliance with Native Americans, and they had over 45,000 troops. The war eventually ended when Washington sent American General "Mad" Anthony Wayne. The general strategically won the decisive Battle of Timbers in 1794.

The latter also involved other nations, but on a much larger scale. The French Revolutionary Wars were a series of wars starting from 1789 until 1799. It was waged with the purposes of expansion of territory by conquest. However, it was derailed by a revolution that began in France itself.

French radicals, led by Napoleon Bonaparte, fought for the liberation of the country from oppressive monarchs. The French called for the involvement of Americans, remembering their friendship during the American Revolution, but Washington took a neutral stance.

Retirement

After serving two terms, Washington resigned from the presidency in March 1797. His farewell address was rife with idealism, republicanism, humility, and gratitude. He was confident in the republic that he was leaving behind. He believed that the foundations it was built upon would be able to withstand anything. Washington, as always, promoted unity. It was necessary to rise above differences in religion and political beliefs and come together as a nation. He made a point to warn against the danger of partisanship and sectionalism. Finally, with utmost sincerity, he thanked the American people for letting him serve them.

The aged hero then returned to Mount Vernon, where he lived out the rest of his days. Washington went back to his simple life of farming, business, and familial duties. One snowy evening on December 12, 1799, he rode horseback to inspect his estate, and returned late to the house. His clothes were wet from the snow, and he had developed a mild cough and sore throat.

Thinking nothing of it, he went to bed. He awoke to severe pain in his throat and difficulty breathing, and his distressed wife called for the family doctors. The doctors tried many emergency practices, but Washington stopped them. He calmly said that he was not afraid to die.

George Washington died a painless death on December 14, 1799, at 67 years old. His last words were, "'Tis well." His wife, Martha Washington, sat transfixed at the foot of the bed. She asked the doctor, "Is he gone?", and the doctor nodded. "'Tis well," she echoed.

His burial was carried out in the same manner that he carried himself while he was alive: with graceful simplicity and elegant dignity. On December 18, he received a proper military burial. The solemn funeral was only open to family, friends, and associates. But when word of his death spread, the entire country mourned. Church bells were rung, government officials wore black, and citizens organized funeral processions. Washington was eulogized by many important figures, such as his successor, President Adams, and more famously, by General Henry Lee.

Chapter 9: Legacy

George Washington left an indelible impression in history. He was the first in many things. He was the first commander-in-chief of the United States Army, the first president of the Continental Congress, and the first president of the United States. Washington understood the responsibilities of being the pioneer. And so, he set precedence for every position he has ever held.

He devoted himself completely to each one of his undertakings. He tried to act with the highest level of honor, morality, and commitment. In his quiet, dignified way, this was his legacy. But history disagrees, and it is firm in its stance that Washington's legacy is grander.

Throughout his presidency, he assumed the role as pater patriae, or the father of the nation. It was a term that was used to refer to him while he was living, and it would be used long after his death. The moniker was appropriate. Though he ruled with stern discipline, he imparted invaluable knowledge and wisdom.

His childlessness made this name a divine irony. Washington himself believed that providence made him unable to father children so that he could father a nation. This idea appealed to Americans who resented the British rule. If Washington did not have a successor, the new republic would not be a dynasty.

It was also said that before there was a flag, Washington was the symbol of the American independence. His name was synonymous to the values that America was founded upon. He represented republicanism, liberation, and nationalism. Washington's image was first lionized by his heroic acts in Delaware and Fort Duquesne. However, many stories about Washington were less fact than fiction.

One such example is a story about a boy and cherry tree. It was said that when Washington was six years old, he cut down his father's cherry tree. When asked about it, the boy admitted the deed and bravely said, "I cannot tell a lie." The story had deep roots in American culture, and for good reason. It displayed the integrity and honesty of Washington, even from an early age. Unfortunately, it was discovered that the story only surfaced in 1806. It was manufactured by biographer Mason Locke Weems to sell more books. He was also responsible for the popular myth of Washington and the silver dollar.

Another legacy that Washington left behind was an honest look at slavery. It was an inhumane institution that he largely benefited from. In his will, he stipulated that his slaves should be freed upon the event of his and his wife's death. His will also stated that elderly slaves and orphans should be supported by the estate. Another provision instructed that the children should be taught to read and write. Washington, like most Americans, had a blind spot for the country's greatest shame. But in the last act of his life, he tried to make amends. He was the first founding father to do so.

Washington left behind many letters, which he organized almost obsessively. He kept his correspondence during his service in the military, the war, and the presidency. It was said that he had written almost 18,000 letters. His wife, Martha, on the other hand, had a different reaction. She was thrust into a public life that she did not particularly consent to. In the later part of her life, she resented the loss of her privacy. She burned all her letters to and from Washington, only leaving three by accident.

Nowadays, Washington's image is in currency, postage stamps, monuments, and paintings. He is also the namesake of the nation's capital, Washington D.C. It is worth discussing how modern Americans see Washington from just these relics. Many know him as the father of the nation and the first president of the United States. Many perceive his actions as imperative to the independence of America. However, others condemn his status as a slave-owner and his part in perpetuating slavery.

It is equally interesting to imagine what Washington would think about modern America. On one hand, he would be disheartened by the continued disunity and bipartisanship. He also would condemn the extent of America's imperialism. Specifically, its imperial hold on developing countries and over-involvement with foreign affairs. On the other hand, Washington would appreciate the longevity of the Constitution and America itself. He would also take pride that America still values freedom and liberty above all else.

Chapter 10: Slavery

History is written by the victors. Time and again, this popular adage proves itself to be true. In the case of America, history was written by powerful men, and they left out some unsavory details. Blind spots maintain the narrative that America is the land of the free. However, in Washington's time, this narrative is only true if you were a white American man.

In seventeenth century colonial Virginia, African slaves outnumbered settlers three to one. Slavery was prominent, normalized, and unquestioned. Many colonists profited from it; and the Washingtons were no exceptions. The normalization of inhumane social practices is a curious thing. In modern times, slavery is incontestably a violation of human rights. But with its legalization, it became a nuanced thing, a gray area, if you will. And there are shades of gray that are darker than others.

George Washington owned slaves for the majority of his life. As he got richer and more powerful, he accumulated more; by the end of his life, he owned 317 adult slaves. It was said that with time and experience, he grew to detest the institution. In his will, he stipulated that in the event of his wife's death, his slaves should be freed. His treatment of the Negroes he owned was indicative of his guilt and ambiguity on the matter. He saw them as properties, but he also recognized their humanity. This belief was contradictory, and as a result, so were his actions.

Washington frequently went to and participated in slave auctions and lotteries. When he purchased slaves, he was partial to strong men and adolescent women. He put up slaves for collateral, and accepted them as payment. In the same way that there is honor among thieves, he tried to have a code as a slave-owner.

First, he cared about their health and welfare. He inoculated his slaves against smallpox. When his slaves were sick, he allowed them to be treated "with tenderness and humanity when sick". He even allowed them to get checked by doctors. Second, he cared about their relationships. He did not sell slaves if it meant that a family would be separated. He also permitted slaves to wed other slaves, even if the marriage is not legally binding. And lastly, he limited the use of whipping. However, in his frequent absence, this was not strictly observed. Perhaps it is because of this code that he can reconcile his fight for freedom while depriving others of it. But this is still problematic; after all, a well-treated slave is still a slave.

Although he emancipated his slaves in his will, it must not be forgotten that, for most of his life, he was a privileged man in a position of power. He was a founding father, a general, a legislator, and a president. In any of those positions, he had the unique opportunity to implement change. He was a man who believed in freedom, equality, and justice; he believed in it so strongly that he fought a war for it. And yet, he allowed for and abetted the continuance of slavery.

It also should be noted that in his life, slavery was not simply a footnote. His small role as a slave-master influenced his greater role as a military officer, a statesman, and a president. His racist bias was not contained to the fact that he owned slaves. He actively passed legislation to allow it to continue, namely the Fugitive Slave Act of 1793.

Although he believed that slavery was immoral and inhumane, he also thought that abolition would collapse the economy. In this respect, Washington is a prime example of the irony and hypocrisy of America.

It is a difficult thing to reconcile such evil with what most perceive was a man of honor. It can be tempting to provide excuses - he was the product of his time, slavery was legal, and he expressed some moral qualms towards the end of his life. But a good analysis of a dead man's character doesn't require one to admire the good and forgive the bad. A good analysis considers both sides, with no intent of admiration or absolution. It acknowledges the merits of the actions and the corruptibility of the motivation. George Washington need not be lauded for his victories, nor redeemed for his failings. In the end, history is not for people to love or condemn; it is for people to learn from.

Chapter 11: Notable Moments

The great and illustrious life of George Washington can be traced to a few important events. His fate was intertwined with that of America's, and so, these moments defined both his life and his nation.

Birth and Early Life

February 22, 1732: George Washington was born to Augustine Sr. and Mary Ball Washington. His birthplace is Westmoreland County, Virginia.

April 12, 1743: Augustine Washington Sr. died. He bequeathed his son, George, ten slaves and Ferry Farm.

1743: He met his half-brother, Lawrence, who married Anne Fairfax. George lived with them in their house in Mount Vernon. Lawrence then introduced him to the Fairfax family. Colonel William Fairfax became George's patron. The colonel's son, George William Fairfax, became one of George's oldest friends.

1746: Lawrence and Colonel Fairfax wanted George to pursue a career in the Navy. His mother, Mary, did not consent.

1748: With that option ruled out, George pursued a career as a land surveyor instead.

1749: George was appointed as the official surveyor of Culpeper, Virginia.

1751: Lawrence contracted tuberculosis and died in the following year on July 26, 1752. According to his will, George was to inherit Mount Vernon in the event that his wife and daughter died.

Virginia Militia

1752: Washington enlisted in the militia. By December, he was appointed as the adjutant of Northern district.

February 1753: He was promoted to major by Lieutenant Governor Robert Dinwiddie. He then assigned Washington to send the French a message, asking them to vacate Ohio County.

January 1754: He submitted a detailed report of the French territory. This served as a confirmation that the French were prepared for war. Washington's report precipitated the French-Indian War, which lasted from 1754 - 1762.

April 2, 1754: Washington perpetrated a deadly attack against a small group of French troops. He believed that the group was a clandestine operation sent to kill them. A French peace envoy was killed in the process, and this caused the French to retaliate.

July 1754: He built Fort Necessity to prepare for the attack, but a third of his troops died. He then surrendered to the French, marking the battle a defeat.

1754: Washington resigned from the military. The French-Indian war was officially declared.

1755: Washington returned to the military to serve as General Edward Braddock's aide. Their mission was to capture Fort Duquesne.

July 9, 1755: The Battle of Monongahela was an ambush, and over two-thirds of the troops were killed. Braddock died four days later.

1758: Washington was promoted to commander-in-chief of Virginia.

1756: He unsuccessfully ran for a seat in the House of Burgesses. He tried again two years later, and he won.

November 1758: Washington successfully captured Fort Duquesne.

December 1758: He resigned his post as commander-in-chief, and went home to Mount Vernon.

Personal Life

1758: George Washington and Martha Dandridge Custis had gotten engaged.

January 6, 1759: The young couple got married at Martha's estate, the White House.

1759: He adopted his wife's son and daughter from her first marriage. The children were Jacky and Patsy, respectively. The family lived in Mount Vernon.

1773: Patsy Custis died from a violent episode of epilepsy.

1773: Jacky Custis married Eleanor Calvert.

After the Militia

1758: He began construction and renovation of the Mount Vernon estate.

1762: Washington served as a vestryman in an Anglican church, and he held this post for twenty years.

February 10, 1763: The Treaty of Paris marked the end of the French-Indian War.

1765: The Stamp Act had passed, and it was met with a wave of violent discontent in the colonies. It was repealed a year later.

1766: The Townshend Act was enacted. Washington advocated for a wide-scale boycott of British goods.

Commander-in-chief

July 17, 1774: Washington and Colonel George Mason penned the Fairfax Resolves. They also established an independent Virginian militia.

August 1774: Washington was selected as a Virginian delegate for the First Continental Congress.

May 1775: The Battle of the Lexington and Concord happened on the eve of the Second Continental Congress. It sparked the beginning of the American Revolutionary War.

July 4, 1776: The Second Continental Congress convened. 39 of 42 delegates signed the Declaration of Independence. Washington was elected as the commander-in-chief.

July 3, 1775: Washington officially assumed command of the United States Army.

December 25, 1775: Washington crossed the Delaware. Despite the harsh weather, he led his troops while incurring no losses.

December 26, 1775: He led a surprise attack on the Hessians. This would later be called the Battle of Trenton, and it was a small but important victory for the Americans.

January 3, 1776: He launched an attack at Princeton and won. 194 British men surrendered.

September 19, 1777: Under Washington's orders, General Gates launched a campaign to attack Saratoga. This decisive battle led to the resignation of the British colonel in charge.

October 19, 1781: Washington successfully sieged Yorktown. This victory led to the signing of the Treaty of Paris in 1783. The treaty marked the end of the American Revolutionary War. Under the treaty, Britain also formally recognized America as an independent country.

1783: Washington resigned as commander-in-chief and disbanded the army. He then went home to Mount Vernon.

Politics

May 25 - September 17, 1787: The Constitutional Convention was held in Pennsylvania. This convention served to rectify the Articles of Confederation. Washington went as a delegate, and was elected the president of the convention.

February 4, 1789: Washington was elected as the first President of the United States. He was inaugurated on April 23 in New York City, and he took oath of office a week later.

August 25, 1789: Mary Ball Washington died from breast cancer.

March 1791: Per Hamilton's proposal, the Congress passed a law to tax whiskey. From 1791 - 1794, it led to an uprising called the Whiskey Rebellion.

February 13, 1793: Washington was sworn into office for his second term.

1793: He signed the Fugitive Slave Act, and the Slave Tract of 1794 one year later.

Resignation

September 19, 1796: Philadelphia papers published Washington's farewell address. He personally read this to the congress on December 7, 1796.

March 1797: Washington resigned from the presidency after his second term. He then returned to Mount Vernon.

December 12, 1799: He experienced a mild sore throat and some difficulty in breathing. His condition rapidly deteriorated over the next two days.

December 14, 1799: George Washington died peacefully in his home in Mount Vernon.

Chapter 12: Trivia

Here are fifteen fun facts you might not know about George Washington.

1. He was not born on February 22. According to Washington family records, he was actually born on February 11, 1732. The recorded date was in accordance with the Julian calendar. His birthdate was deferred when Britain's colonies followed the Gregorian calendar.

2. Many people might assume that he wore a wig, but Washington was actually a natural redhead. He powdered his hair white, as was fashionable at the time.

3. When Washington died in 1799, his rank was Lieutenant General of the United States Army. But in 1976, President Gerald R. Ford thought that Washington's actions should be held in the highest regard. He posthumously appointed Washington as the General of the Armies of the United States, the highest rank in American history.

4. The most respected general in history actually lost more battles than he won. Washington fought in the French-Indian War, American Revolutionary War, and the Quasi war. The battles of Fort Necessity, Monongahela, Long Island, and White Plains were all defeats. As a commanding officer, his total tally was eight defeats, six victories.

5. He was the only US president to lead troops into war while in office. This was during the Whiskey Rebellion of 1791.

6. Washington was not a particularly devout person. But, interestingly, many people believed that he was protected by divine providence. This is due in large part to his actions during Braddock's exhibition. He heroically crossed a brutal battleground while ill. Yet, somehow, he avoided sustaining any injury whatsoever. He escaped unscathed, with no less than four bullet holes in his clothes, two in his hat, and two dead horses.

7. Although he was not religious, he strongly advocated for religious tolerance. He mentioned 22 major churches, denominations, and religious groups in his presidential addresses.

8. Washington was among the strongest, most formidable presidents, but he was also the sickliest. He survived a great deal of deadly illnesses – smallpox, pleurisy, tuberculosis, malaria, diphtheria, dysentery, and pneumonia. He eventually died from epiglottitis and respiratory infection.

9. It was largely speculated that his poor health caused his infertility. It was one of life's greatest ironies – that the father of America was in fact, childless.

10. Washington strongly disapproved of a partisan government. He believed that it would promulgate division, dissent, and disunity. He feared that it would present a threat of loyalty to party over country.

11. He was plagued by dental problems his whole life, and so he rarely, if at all, smiled with teeth. Washington was so conscious about his teeth that when he wrote to his dentist, he used euphemisms. At the time of his presidency, he only had one tooth left. However, contrary to popular belief, his teeth were made from ivory, not wood.

12. He was a dog lover who owned as many as fifty dogs. He was formally credited for developing a breed named the American foxhound. The foxhound is also the state dog of Virginia, his hometown.

13. During the battle of Germantown, he found a dog running loose on the battlefield. According to its collar, it was owned by a general on the opposing side. He brought the dog into his tent, fed it, bathed it, and brushed it. He then ordered a ceasefire, so the dog could return to its owner.

14. As the leader of a new government, his officials and constituents were unsure how to address him. He believed that

the presidency shouldn't have the airs of the monarchy, and so he landed on the title "Mr. President."

15. Washington and his family never actually occupied the White House. However, his wife, Martha Washington, owned an estate coincidentally named the White House.

Conclusion

Thanks again for taking the time to read this book!

You should now have a good understanding of George Washington, and the incredible life he lived.

If you enjoyed this book, please take the time to leave me a review on Amazon. I appreciate your honest feedback, and it really helps me to continue producing high quality books.

CPSIA information can be obtained
at www.ICGtesting.com
Printed in the USA
BVHW042308070719
552809BV00013B/793/P

9 781925 989403